Slow Love & Faded Scars
Copyright © Anne Robson 2018

All rights reserved. No part of this book may be reproduced or transmitted in any form or by any means without written permission from the author.

A catalogue record for this book is available from the National Library of Australia

Published in Australia

ISBN 978-0-646-98375-2

Anne Robson
www.annerobson.com.au

Book and cover design by Alana Maybus
www.alanamaybus.com

Slow Love & Faded Scars

Anne Robson

Dedication

*To everyone who put up with me during the writing of this book
and to anyone who puts up with me now it's published.
A never-ending thank you to my family for their solid support,
and to Roger and Harry, whom I hold responsible for the final result.*

*Alana Maybus, you have unlimited patience!
Your design is a thing of beauty.*

Contents

Scar Lines

Morning	14
Magnificent	15
Crying	16
No One Dies Until They Are Forgotten	18
Hail To The Bottle	21
Loss & Renewal: A Tale In Haiku	22
I Thought I Knew Love	25
Set Kindness Free	26
The Wrongdoer	28
Envy	29
The Photo	30
Becoming You	32
Only Then Did I Realise	34
Jealousy	35
Talking To Ants	36
Sweat	38

Slow Love & Memories

Cracks	42
Erosion	43
The Moan	44
The Kiss	45
The Ending	46
Steal Away	48
Beautiful	49
Like A Full Blown Rose	50
Reconnection	51
The Stranger	52
Courage	53
Slow Love And Faded Scars	55

Wounded	56
The Cock Crows	57
You	58
Pain	59
Earl Grey Tea	60
I Think This Might Be love	62
I'm Your Storm	63
Go Out And Love	64
Gossip	65
The Icing On The Cake	66
He Loves Me	68
You Are My Sin	69

Stories Of Life & Love

Moving On	72
A Time To Leave	75
Lady Of The Night	76
No Bruises To Show	78
The Virgin	82
An Affair	84
Winters Tale	86
Twisted Murder	88
Pregnancy	92
Grandma Loves You	94
My Weakness	96
Laundry Day	100
The Superiority Of Men	102
African Queen	105

Scar Lines

Morning.

Untangling entwined limbs,
sliding my fingers along the landscape of your spine,
pulling you close, face to face, skin to skin.

Kissing words of love into your welcoming lips,
gently parting them,
probing deeper,
my first morning breath is yours.

Inviting passion, our slowly opening eyes begin to
dance together like wanton spirits,
speaking without words.

Enveloped in the weight of your arms, your body,
your safety, your heat, morning bursts into me as
the dawn breaks.

Magnificent.

If you only knew how much I believe in you.
If you only knew the faith I have in you.
If you could see yourself through my eyes,
You would never doubt yourself again.
Let me be your mirror, clear and true.
Let me show you the man I see.

You are the strength and the beauty
That daily fills my world.
You are the love and honesty
I rely on to keep me balanced.
You are my adventure and my sanctuary,
My wildness and my peace.

You are my creative spark
And caretaker of my imagination.
You are my softness
And you are my power.
You are my heart, my magnificent man.

Crying Out Loud.

Tears are classified as acceptance.
It doesn't matter what you say.
By virtue of your weakness,
They find a way to make you pay.

Pinned down naked in groaning dark,
A sprawl of hate across my face,
I cry out loud against the dawn
And memories I can't erase.

Lewd conversations lurk in the halls.
Judgement drips from every word.
Dress them up in kind concern
As though the words had gone unheard

Head held high and shoulders back,
Vitriolic fury drives my brain.
Graffiti smiles tattoo my face.
I'm a savage angel, deep in pain.

No One Dies Until They Are Forgotten.

They say she died a few years ago,
But still he's married to her.
Faithful yet to the woman he adored.
Wearing the wedding ring she long ago
slipped onto his finger.

No one dies until they are forgotten.
And she lives on,
Embedded in his life from morning 'til night.
Still she dances in his dreams.
And he talks with her in his thoughts each day.

It's such a beautiful love.
Magical and hard to find.
It's how I want to be loved.
To be loved by him.

But she is the fence around his heart.
It seems impossible to scale.
I can't replace her.
And I don't want her to be forgotten.

I will celebrate her with him.
I will listen to his memories,
And hold him when he grieves.
If he would only allow an opening in that fence.
Just a small one.
Just enough for me.

Hail To The Bottle.

Another day, another bottle.
You'd think I could do without it.
But it soothes me.
Saviour of my day,
Demon slayer of my night.
All hail liquor,
Water of the soul.

Oh, delicious wine.
Succulent grapes of ruby power.
Fill me like a vessel.
Tip your angelic peace
Into my weary mind.
Keep the stress of life at bay
Until the bottle's dry.

You can demonise me.
"Drink dependant and weak."
But I don't want any pedestal.
And I'm not lost.
I know exactly who I am.
I'm sodden-veined,
And wholly unrepentant.

Loss and Renewal.
A Tale in Haiku.

Break Up
Wilting in the dust
Discovered in betrayal
Soiled love lies broken

Despair
Despair and regret
Spikes of loss puncture each day
A lament of pain

Autopilot
Mute, blinded and numb
There suspended on keen wires
Hangs my acid heart

Recovery
Gentle velvet tip
Soft green bud of renewal
Sees the world as new

Hope
I wait in patience
Hoping you will notice me
Behind my disguise

Celebration
I caught you, wild heart
Remote and rugged you were
Now you are all mine

Renewal
Truly do I love
Embrace and hold with full heart
New life in my arms

I Thought I Knew Love.

I thought I knew love.
But never have I felt fingers of emotion dig into me with such savagery,
nor felt the shockwaves zapping up my spine.

Never have I been short of breath just thinking of a man, nor struggled to control sudden urges to escape to him.
To leave my life behind; to risk everything for just one lover.

But for you I am willing to discard my world.
I will run with you into the unknown.
And never look back.

Set Kindness Free.

Kindness slips in on soft falling feet,
And stands unnoticed in the crowd.
With silent eyes and muted face,
She waits in patience for the call.
There's a desolate soul nearby,
Splattered in fierce bravado.
And none shall see, none shall know,
How deep the need inside.

Who will recognise kindness
If not someone she knows well?
Who has felt her saving touch
When it was needed most.

Kindness comes and doesn't leave.
You meet her and she's yours.
Not to keep, but to share.
She's in your hands and in your eyes.
She's in the way you lead,
Stumbling towards peace.

Listen up and heed the call.
You are her chosen vessel,
And a desolate soul awaits.
All you need is what you've got,
So open up and set kindness free.

The Wrongdoer.

My heart is a catacomb,
My mind its neurotic wanderer.
Pacing out the passages
And poking into the dead,
It searches out old mistakes.
Finding reasons to beat myself
As I shrivel in remorse
For deeds long past.

The more it pokes, the more it finds.
My sins prattle in the dark,
Spilling their dirty little secrets.
In my head, noises vibrate,
A maelstrom of guilt
Spinning in my skull.
A perfectionate discord
Of spitting sibilance.

Like a bonefish on mudflats
The mind pounces on its prey,
Feeding its neuroses
With fat, juicy lies.
Waspishness becomes me,
Deflects friends and foe.
I'm a tomb that walks
With punishment in tow.

Envy.

Envy is a pure beast,
A mean and poisonous art
That plots and writes the future.
Calligraphy with iron heart.

A holey soul is riddled.
The caterpillar boarder
Leaves stains of jaundiced lust.
Another sin to launder.

No seamstress can repair
What envy tears apart.
No placebo can relieve
The pain of envy's art.

The offspring is the sin,
Hard, colourful and wild.
Improvisation screwed.
Now envy has a child.

The Photo.

How will I forget you
When a glance at your photo
Still hits me with shock?
Those wild days after,
When I did random things
In random ways
To make me feel again.
Something...
Anything...
They're still inside me.
I can't let them go.
It's unresolved.
I'm unresolved.
You cut me.
Your look and your word,
Both sharp and deadly.
You didn't have to do it that way.
You could have just walked out the door.
You could have just said goodbye.
You should have just gone.
You found my soft spot.
You lacerated me
With polite dismissal.
Who could ever follow that?
I'll never be whole again.
My heart lies blooded on the ground.
Yours is already at the airport.

Becoming You.

If you stand still long enough
You grow to be invisible.
Blotted from human consciousness
Like a streetlamp in the light of day.

No one asks your opinion.
They know what you're going to say.
They just work around you
As if you aren't there.

You're just you,
The same you that you've always been
Even if, on the inside,
You know you've changed.

Becoming someone new
Isn't just about changing your mindset.
It's about taking up new spaces
And learning how to move.

Don't just stand there.
Feel your blood bubbling inside.
It won't let you stand still any more.
You're claiming a new space.

Feel your soul peeling back your skin
And forcing its way out into the world.
It's the birth of a person.
And you are a revelation.

Only Then Did I Realise.

Why didn't I see it then?
Why didn't I realise?
I knew my skin sang when you touched me
By accident as we passed by.

I knew I skipped a breath
When we leant close to work.
I swear I saw your heart beating
As my eyes crept down your shirt.

It was too late when I knew.
You were gone and I was empty.
When you found her.

Only then did I realise.

Jealousy.

I'm jealous of the swirling breeze
That teases you in ways I cannot.
Rustling under the hair at the nape of your neck,
Slipping inside your shirt
And fingering your soft skin.

I'm jealous of the radiant sun
That heats your blood in ways I cannot.
Lingering on your face, your skin,
Shining life into your eyes
And warming your beloved body.

I'm jealous of the streaming water
That plays with your nakedness in ways I cannot.
Caressing your form with absolute intimacy,
Trickling into your secret places
And renewing your sacred soul.

Talking To Ants.

Sunlight breaks into the blushing sky.
Puts a flush of colour on the earth nearby.
I lie face down in the common grass
And mumble to the ants that pass.

I tried to steal my love away,
To take his heart with fake displays
Of qualities I did not own
And promises of sweet unknowns.

With muscle tense, I feel the guilt.
With open palms feel tears that spilt.
I've bought my way to lonely soil,
Escaping shame and stark turmoil.

The ants ignore my sad distress
And do their work with pure finesse.
I've dug my life into a hole.
My world is now beyond control.

Sweat.

It's 40 degrees outside.
Indoors, our only relief is the fan,
Spitting and hissing as it overheats,
Agitating from side to side.

We lie on the exhausted bed
Caught in sodden, tangled sheets
Which fought us all night
As we sought the missing sleep.

I can hear a blowfly
Buzzing and banging on the window.
It's the only creature moving
In the heat-laden afternoon stillness.

The fan spurts a welcome breeze
Randomly strewn across our bodies.
From the corner of my eye I see
His body limp but his nipples alive
Celebrating the moving air.

Sweat beads have settled on his chest
Sparkling in the fading light.
One bead moves, sinuously sliding
Into the valleys of his chest.

A beautiful shimmering droplet forms
As one bead joins another,
Slipping further down his body,
Gaining speed and urgency,
Begging me to follow.

But it's deceptive.
Sweat offers no slip.
Our skins are sticky.
Pinching together like a Chinese burn,
There is no relief anywhere.

Slow Love & Memories

Cracks.

You don't love a man because he is a perfect human being. You love him because he is not. All those imperfections are the spices that give him his unique flavour. And all those cracks are simply openings into which you can inject your healing love.

Erosion.

Some days I wake up and I'm in a retrospective mood. I don't know why it happens, but it isn't always a blessing. Sometimes my mind is filled with regrets for the things I have done or not done, and the thoughts slow me down all day. They drip through my fingers and into my writing. They drip onto my tongue and into the words I speak. They drip into my soul and make it weak. They drip constantly, eroding everything I do and everything I am.

The Moan.

I took him by surprise, cupping him gently before he woke. Morning's slow love is hot love. A sweet, gentle glide. And his moan escaped before his eyes were even open.

The Kiss.

I'd forgotten what it was like to be kissed. Really kissed. Kissed into the depths of your soul. I'd forgotten how the world stops, and there's nothing but silence all around. How all you can hear is the thudding of your heart's powerful rhythm. And all you can feel are those passionate lips pulling the heart right out of your body.

The Ending.

I knew it would end. I knew you couldn't be mine forever.

I know you loved me. But you loved her, too.
I gave you everything I could give. My heart.
My soul. My body. I even gave you my dignity.
I gave until there was nothing left to give. Yet I still couldn't give you enough. I couldn't give you whatever she gives.

I told myself I would let you go without a whimper, yet I didn't count on the torment I'd feel. On the overwhelming and torturous despair, knowing you were choosing her over me.

But would I love you all over again?
In a heartbeat.

For a while there, I really lived.

Steal Away.

Steal away with me. Creep with me out of this caged world. Get lost with me. Stretch those cramped limbs. Release your heart and your mind. Steal away with me. Rediscover your wildness. Be my untamed lover, as I will be yours.

Beautiful.

You are very beautiful, but you don't even know it. That's not what you see when you look in the mirror. You see the young man has gone, and in his place is a man with grey hair and rounded belly. But I see humour, intelligence, eyes I could drown in. I see honour and dignity. And I see your pure soul. Yet you'll never notice me over here admiring you because you don't even know to look.

Like a Full-Blown Rose.

One day you will come across a man who revels in your essence. Who sees you fully and completely, sees your purity and even your darkness, yet chooses to stay. That is when you come alive, your perfume scenting every day, your petals stretching towards him as though he is the sun and you a full-blown rose.

Reconnection.

We recognised each other straight away. We are the same people we used to be. The same hearts and the same souls still beat inside us, despite the scattering years. We touch, needing no hands nor bodies to reach each other deep inside. Neither time nor distance will stop the rekindling of our relationship. For we know that in each other lies the rediscovery of the missing; the art of living and the art of passion.

The Stranger.

His sunbaked fingers trailed round the perimeter of her lips with a familiarity no stranger should have. She lay on the bed, her body a landscape of contrasts, at once known and unknown to him. Arching her back, she stretched sensuously, her actions directing his gaze towards the bare skin of her belly. She reached out and touched the tight, white curls that swathed his head like lamb's wool. He was no challenge to her. With supreme confidence, she pulled him towards her, and took him deep into the swamp of blankets and passion.

Courage.

What am I afraid of? I've never been able to make a decision when it really counts. I don't allow myself the space to explore, or the freedom to take a risk. I don't give myself the forgiveness I give others if they make a mistake. No mea culpa for me, and no Confiteor. Like a coward, I put the reins of my life into the hands of another, and must live with the consequences.

Slow Love and Faded Scars.

Sometimes we hurtle headlong into passion. A world painted in eye-popping colours. The blood in our veins heating until it bubbles. Yes, we might end up burnt and sometimes even scarred. But oh, what a freeform and turbulent ride it is discovering a delirious, heady joy never to be forgotten.

But slow love is a sneaky love, building to a peak without battles and drama. Taking you by surprise. Serene and gentle, it recognises the beauty of your faded love scars, each one a moment of past glory. It binds them into you and makes you whole.

Don't mistake slow love's quiet arrival as passionless. Intensity burns silently. Slow love is your healer and your completion.

Wounded.

Blood dries fast on the skin.
Faster without,
Than the wound within,
Still seeping after all this time.

The Cock Crows.

She heard the cock crow, and knew he was calling for her. Standing tall and proud, puffed up with his strong sense of manhood, he demanded she come down from the fence. The hay was beckoning; as powerful a call to her needs as was his persistence. Yet she knew she could only keep his attention for a short while before he began to strut elsewhere. Bringer of love and maker of despair, she finally succumbed to him, knowing that tears would follow.

Slow Love & Memories

You.

You. It's such a small word. Inoffensive, and one we can apply to anyone.

You. Could you please put out the rubbish? Are you free for a quick chat? Would you mind...

But You.

When did You become a way of life?
You the person. You the mind. You the soul and spirit. You the ethereal heart. You with your history and your baggage. You with your love. And You, the warm being I hold in my arms, strong and firm and real.

I love You.

You are a world, not a word.

Pain.

I can feel pain inside me.
Like a hot ball of molten wax,
Always changing its shape.

Earl Grey Tea.

"He likes Earl Grey tea," she whispers to me as her faded eyes scan the horizon.

I fill the kettle and place it to boil.
Gripping my arm with a sense of urgency, she says again, "He likes Earl Grey tea."

"That's OK, Nana. We have Earl Grey tea."

As I have done every morning for many years now, I brew three cups of steaming tea, leaving one to cool on the counter, ready for the man who will never come home.

I Think This Might Be Love.

I run to you because when I'm in your arms, you take me where I need to go. You calm my fears, soothe my battered feelings, and give me the nourishment I need to keep going. You alone know the right words and how to say them. And honestly? I choose to believe, not even knowing whether or not you really mean them. I think at last this might be love.

I'm Your Storm.

Life with me won't be easy.
I'm your storm, and I'm your sunshine.

I'm your hunger, and I'm your feast.
I'm your power, and I'm your weakness.

If you stay with me, one thing's for sure.
You will know what it's like to be well
and truly loved.

Slow Love & Memories

Go Out and Love.

It's not more things we need to be happy in our worlds. It's more love. Go out and love someone. Change the world—one hug, one kiss, one love at a time. And with that one hug you'll find, like a two-for-one deal, your world starts to change too.

Gossip.

Anyone can post a comment to the world without fear of the trash basket. It can't be stopped. No such thing as pending gossip. No one needs to approve it. It's out there straight away. You just roll it out, and it collects more and more users on the way. Whisper about things that shouldn't be known and wring assumptions from nothing more than appearance. Gossip doesn't need to be justified. Just sit at your dashboard of destruction and pick a target. There's no anti-spam program for gossip.

The Icing on The Cake.

Sex and desire are the icing on the cake. But who wants the icing alone? I want all of you, just as you are. In the body you've been given. With your caring soul. With your generous and loving heart. With those eyes that see things in me no one else ever has. I want the you that loves me as I am. I love the icing, but it's the cake I want. You are my cake, and I want it all.

He Loves Me.

"You are the moon beneath which I dance naked and worship. You are the purity of the waters in which I bathe, and the soil wherein lies planted the seed of our love." Yes, that's how I know he loves me.

You Are My Sin.

You are my sin. You are my addiction. I need to be tangled in you, feeling your hand at the nape of my neck, your hot lips kissing my throat. I cannot get enough of you. And, remorseless, I want those heady, breathless sins to pile up. When you're not here, I shoot up with them while dreaming of sinning again.

Stories Of Life & Love

Moving On.

The gusty winds of change burst forcefully through the wilderness of her thoughts, and she inhaled hungrily.
"Sell up. Move on. Become free."

The chant drummed through her brain over and over again, getting faster and faster, racing her heartbeat to the finish line.

She was done with them all. Done with their suspicious minds, and grasping fingers as sticky as toffee where money was concerned.

"Sell up. Move on. Become free."

The colour of freedom was beginning to paint itself across the canvas of her monotone world. She sat on the window ledge, looking out towards the bay. The moon shimmered on the damp sand, creating the illusion of a pathway to the water's edge.

Freedom was just ahead. But she knew that whatever she did now would have immense consequences. It was time to dissolve her gentle soul and give birth to the warrior woman inside.

With only a change of clothes in her backpack she stood looking out the window. The tree was beyond arm's reach, and the drop below was scary. But the warrior woman pushed her from deep inside. Scrambling through the window, she balanced on the ledge.

And, drawing one huge breath, she leapt towards her future.

A Time To Leave.

When is it OK to admit you're not happy? To tell him you need to get away, expand your boundaries and breach your limits?

Even before I say anything I can picture the expression on his face.

The hurt.
The pain.
The accusation.

OK, maybe he's right. Maybe it is all my fault that we're in this situation. But he's been avoiding this conversation for a long time now. His head has been more firmly in the ground than any ostrich could mimic.

Of course, he'd tell me ostriches don't really do that. That it's an urban myth and I'm wrong. I'm always wrong.
And I can't take it anymore.

I used to be bright and intelligent. I had opinions once, and was even happy to share them. But slowly, in his subtle way, he's squeezed it all out of me. I didn't even notice it happening. Life, kids, work, Oh how things can change when you're not paying attention.

I don't think I can wait any longer.
After all, what am I really waiting for?

Lady Of The Night.

Her dress was damp and spotted with mould. But under the lamplight it looked fine.

Hell, she was sick of the humidity. And the storms! Sitting in darkness night after night, no power to even turn her fan.

Outside was no better. The pavement was steaming after the rain and the air was hot and heavy in her throat. Her clothes clung to her like a punch-drunk boxer, petticoats wrapping around her legs as she walked.

It was so still and quiet. Many of her neighbours had come outdoors to escape the suffocating heat of their apartments. Wilted and tired, they sat motionless beneath the gaze of the old building they lived in.

She looked wistfully look in a dress shop window, imagining herself wearing something so fine without having to endure the chemical smell that scented her clothes to keep them mould-free.

A sigh inserted itself into the already heavy air.

Resigned to her situation, she continued on in the accepted format of her night, smiling boldly at the gentlemen she passed.

No Bruises to Show.

If anyone bothered to look into her eyes, they'd see they were uninhabited.

If they bothered to listen to her words, they'd notice she never gave a clear answer.

If they ever stopped long enough to watch her, they'd wonder about her skittishness—the way her eyes constantly slid towards her man, tracking his location in the surroundings.

She had no bruises to show for his abuse, so perhaps it wasn't real. Maybe it was all in her imagination. People told her how lucky she was to have such a caring partner. And as they did he'd smile and slip his arm firmly around her waist, pulling her close in ownership.

Perhaps he didn't mean it, as he sat with his face in the shadows, when he said he was leaving her and taking everything. Without seeing his face, there were no clues to go by. The nerves in her gut made her feel sick.

Perhaps he didn't mean it when he threw that glass of beer into her face in public, blaming her for three droplets of alcohol that had landed on his head from out of nowhere. And then angrily telling her she smelt like a bar room whore as they drove home.

Perhaps he didn't mean it when he said she could never have a male friend, and lurked outside her workplace to see who she spoke to as she left the building.

Perhaps he didn't mean it when he shouldered her into the wall that night after his mate put an arm around her, demanding that she shower and disinfect. Or when he pushed her so far away from him that she almost fell out of the car door as they drove along the highway. (There were bruises that time.)

But she knew he meant it when he threatened to harm her if she was ever unfaithful to him. He went into that in graphic detail.

She no longer owned anything. He took care of it all.
She had learned never to make a decision without consulting him first. After all, it was his decision that counted.

If she needed money—money that she'd worked hard for—she needed to beg for it, and justify the need.

She'd also learned never to ask for help, for he had ways of finding out. No friends ever came to visit. She no longer had any.
He'd made sure of that.

He was an angry man, often without reason, and he took his anger out on her. She'd sit as he spewed his anger all over her, never allowed to leave her seat until he'd finished.

But she had no bruises to show, so everything must be OK, right?

The Virgin

Her bedroom was a mess.

The bedcovers were askew, and items of clothing were scattered around the carpet like confetti. The last rays of the November sun curled around the curtains, falling on her like a spotlight.

She had the bed to herself now. Her playmate had gone back to his class. She remembered him looking at her, eyes filled with accusation and a forced smile of happiness on his lips.

The strange contradiction excited her, and she almost wished he'd come back. Even his lack of patience was promising.

Society frowned on it, of course. Her peers would never understand her love of virgins.

She'd discovered that 18 was the perfect age for them to start playing. She wanted the rights to their lean and muscly bodies. She wanted to be the one introducing them to pleasure, breaking them in like young stallions. She wanted the innocence-flavoured lips and the tentative kisses of lustful beginners.

But there was no rush. This one was good. A little play here, a little tease there. Let him leave wanting more. He'd be back and then she would take him further and further.

Ah, she loved virgins. Part toy, part pure satisfaction.

An Affair.

It was hot. And it was wild.

Insatiable, they couldn't stay apart. Clothes strewn across the floors and furniture, they abandoned themselves to each other whenever time could be stolen from the real world.

His was the stake on which she burned—risking everything, yet unable to keep away. Hers were the flames that engulfed him, charring him on the cross whenever they were together.

The clock was their enemy. Silently counting down, converting their moments of rampant passion into dull units of time. It was the only material element of the outside world they allowed to intrude on their privacy. Like the opinionated opponent it was, the clock announced the end of their time in a strident, insistent voice.

For every high there's a low, and theirs was deep and ferocious. Like two halves of the page they tore themselves apart, feeling every centimetre of the wound searing their scorched skins.

He dragged his satiated body back to lead the evening service. Hand in hand with her husband, she wore shuttered eyes to the church. And during the service the altar candles burnt brighter and stronger, acknowledging the presence of far superior flames.

Winters Tale.

Hail is pounding down outside my fogged-up window, beating my garden into submission with its ferocity.
There's a certain comfort in being huddled into my blanket, even though the cold still dances around the fringes.

A log moves on the fire, sending sparks showering upwards to catch the warm air current before they disappear into the unknown. I'd have welcomed that flicker of heat on my skin. What a waste.

This winter is a test for many. We've become attached to the easy life, and having to make do without power is challenging our habits. We can't just flick a switch to see light or feel warmth. Instead we must block out the cold with thick window coverings, and stuff rags under the doors to keep out the draughts. Nothing seems to save my fingers from the icy bite.

It's a profound change to the way we live. And while the outages don't last long they keep coming around. And I seem to be without power more often than most. I'd welcome the warmth of another body next to mine, but there's no-one here. He left me behind when he moved.

Outside the wind begins to pick up pace, and the hail responds in excitement. I wish the hands on the clock would pick up their pace, too.

Twisted Murder.

She drove madly through the night. Her car was a marlinspike, dividing the strands of past and future as she headed north.

Escape. It was all she could think of.

The moonlight spurted though the bush, leaving stains of light on the road. It was hard to see, but that didn't slow her down.

Ahead of her was a new life and freedom. And she wanted to get there as soon as possible.

She pushed harder on the pedal, and watched the line on her speedo climb. The moonlight strobed as the trees got bigger and the branches leaned drunkenly overhead.
It was a perfect night for a little hoodoo.

Turning on the radio for company, she sang along happily until the alliterative sounds of Better Be a Better Boy got on her nerves. Pushing at the buttons searching for something less mundane to listen to she stumbled across Esoteric. The rich sounds rang out into the night, and she laughed at the humour of listening to a doom band.

She pulled in at the all-night café and grabbed a coffee. The car looked even more jaded than she did, as though it wasn't really enjoying the adventure. She thumped on the boot as she went past and muttered, "Cantankerous old bugger. I hope you're enjoying the trip."

The squeal of her tyres as she hit the bitumen again spoiled the silence of the night. She sped through town after town, marvelling that she hadn't caught the attention of the cops. Just before dawn she turned off the main road and into a side track that wound through the scrub. Her excitement was building.

She could feel the devil in her smile.

Climbing out of the car, she skipped through the dust to the back of her car and thumped on the boot.

"Honey, we're home," she whispered, then tossed her head back in laughter. It was the end of the road at last. She hit a button on the remote, and the boot popped ajar.

Nothing happened.

She waited until she couldn't take it anymore. She bent over, raised the boot, and peered at the body curled up in the cramped space.

He looked dead.

But there was nothing dead about the pistol pointed at her face.

"Who's the victim now, honey?"

The car drove off just as the sun began to rise. The road was free, and so was he. Stretching out his legs, he made himself comfortable for the journey ahead.

Pregnancy.

You need to understand how it feels when your body doesn't belong to you anymore.

In the beginning, it's home to an alien being that has invaded your once private and personal space, and keeps stretching it to fit. Every day you notice a new change in the body you once knew so well.

And I'm not just talking about your belly. Your breasts swell and become tender.

Your feet swell, and start arguing with your shoes. Your fingers swell, quickly rejecting their rings. Your hair won't do what it used to. And your mind wanders until some days you think you've lost it completely.

Piece by piece, your body changes until you've forgotten what normal even was.

Then your alien emerges, and takes up residence on the outside. It hangs from your breast, sleeps in your bed, and demands constant attention. Some days you wish you could put it back on the inside. At least it was quiet there.

And you know that you never get your body back, don't you?

You wait patiently for the alien to grow up. But even as they enter adulthood, you still belong to them. Somehow that umbilical cord is still there, and every time your alien moves you can feel it tug. The more aliens you've carried, the more you're pulled around. They rarely coordinate their needs.

It's no wonder you end up so out of shape. You look in the mirror, and the person looking back is nothing like the one she used to be. She's misshapen, saggy and a little overweight.

But if you look very closely, you'll see a happy soul shining out of those slightly droopy and bleary eyes.

Perhaps the price of a reshaped body isn't too much to pay after all.

Grandma Loves You.

With all the love and concern of a psychopath, she ignored his weakness and carried on walking.

"Hurry up," his grandmother called over her shoulder as she strode purposefully onward. "I don't want my wine to get warm."

The day was hot and dry, and the wind stung as it blew past his bare legs. Leaves blew along the footpath and into the gutters where they lay in wait, their cockeyed serrations ready to scratch bare feet.

He'd waited for her outside the Jubilee Hotel for an hour in the heat while she drank with her cronies inside. He'd hoped it would be enough to put her in a good mood for a while. But she'd bought a bottle out with her, and he knew he was in for a hard time.

With any luck she'd pass out and he'd be free for a while.

He glanced surreptitiously at the people watching him struggle. He could feel their empathy, but knew none of them could break him free of his prison.

His arms grew tired as he lugged the shopping and her precious wine bottle. His legs weren't long enough to keep pace with hers, and he looked ahead at the broad figure of his grandmother. Her rear end shuddered like softened quark inside her jersey pants. She looked harmless – soft grey hair and flapping pink cardigan – but he knew better.

He knew how much trouble he'd be in if the wine lost its chill. He tried calculating how time and distance would affect chill factor, but his mind was too busy dealing with the flutter of anxiety in his chest.

My Weakness.

It was a fancy spread, with cupcakes and parfait glasses sitting side by side. The table was a mass of colours and calories. In the middle was the star of the day—a pineapple cake, complete with its green crown, reigning supreme like a pterodactyl guarding its spoils.

I looked longingly at the chocolate mousse cake. My lips could already feel that velvety richness sliding into tastebud heaven.

"Mum, do you want to share a dessert?" asked my elfin daughter with the elfin appetite.

Share? When it comes to chocolate and dessert that word isn't in my vocabulary.

With a little leverage from the arm of my elfin but surprisingly strong daughter, I managed to excavate my rear end from the chair.

I stood, armed and ready to attack the dessert table with gusto. With an elbow here and a hip bump there I was soon at the head of the queue.

"Aren't people nice?" I said to my daughter, who for some reason was standing a little further away from me.
No response. Humph.

I picked up a bowl and spoon, and started trawling the table for chocolate delicacies. The pterodactyl guarding the table put me off a little, but not enough to dampen my appetite.

I've perfected a technique that allows me to crush huge serves into my bowl without being obvious. I quickly stuffed it with the remaining serves of mousse cake and made it back to my table.

I couldn't wait to taste the delicious layers of chocolate cake and chocolate mousse.

I pulled up my chair, and lowered myself carefully into it. Suddenly I felt myself flopping to the ground, hitting the floor with a thud.

How embarrassing.

Worse still, my bowl fell with me and landed upside down in the lap of my favourite blue dress.

Not the mousse cake! I've been waiting for it all night.

Conscious of everyone looking at me, I slid my hand out to the fallen spoon and grasped it securely, bringing it back to the mess in my lap.

They didn't think I'd waste it, did they?

Laundry Day.

She shook the sheet thoroughly and began pegging it to the clothes line. The wind beat wildly and she struggled as the sheet whipped back and forth. The weather was grim, but it looked like the rain would hold off for a while.

Overhead, a speck in the wild grey sky came closer. First one, then two, and then an entire flock of birds flew overhead, seeking shelter in the nearby trees. She bent to the laundry basket and pulled out another sheet.

A jovial warble came from the treetops.

"What are you so happy about?" she muttered to herself.

Her fingers were sore and her wrists were tired from fighting against sheets that wanted to fly off in the wind.

The birds kept on laughing. At last the laundry was pegged out and flapping freely on the line.

She noticed a vein snaking its way down one sheet. Stepping closer, she spied a doughy mess at the top of one sheet, and the vein bleeding downwards.

Stupid birds! No wonder they were laughing.

She was tired. All her energy had been sapped in the fight against nature. And now it looked as if nature was having the last laugh.

Suddenly, she stepped up to the line and ripped off the pegs. Tugging at the sheet, she set it free. It flapped and turned like a whirlwind off into the grey void overhead.

And as she watched the sheet escaping on its adventure, she felt a twinge of jealousy.

Ah, well. Back to the laundry.

The Superiority of Men.

I gave it a good shake, but the stupid thing refused to open. Since when did resealable bags put up such a fight, anyway?

"Honey? Have a quick search for the scissors, will you?"

"You don't need scissors," he said. "Here, let me show you how to do it."

With a smirk on his face and superiority in his voice, he held out his hand. I thrust the bag at him and turned back to cut up the rest of the ingredients for the salad.

Was that a slight curse I heard? I peeped slyly in his direction. A slight red rising in the cheeks?

A whistle of exasperation emerged from his not-so-superior-now lips, and it was my turn to smirk.

"Well, we might have to do without it," I said, sick of the whole thing. "I guess we don't need it anyway. The pasta will be just as good without it."

I could have sworn I heard him mutter something under his breath about food to kill.

"Well, darling. Perhaps a little bellyache might motivate you to cook for once."

Another chance for me to smirk and feel superior. He couldn't even make toast without burning it.

You'll be pleased to know the pasta was delicious, and later I took my revenge on that bag. Scissors can be really handy sometimes.

That bag will never fight me again.

African Queen.

She looked a little overblown in her black and white striped jumpsuit. But she still had something that anchored a man's eyes.

Billy watched as her generous hips moved in time with the music. She really was one good looking woman. If you liked the African Queen type. He took another swig from his bottle, struggling to stay vertical on the chair. It wasn't the liquor that was affecting him. It was the sheer exhaustion and tropical heat pounding through his body.

The rhythm of the drum thundered in his head and the sound dripped, bleeding from his ears. If this relationship was to continue, he knew one of them would have to convert— he to the music or she to the silence.

The beat shifted and slowed, but the rapid pulse inside his brain only accelerated. She was looking directly at him. Her body slowed to a sway, and those stellar eyes needled into him, pinning him to the chair like a moth to a specimen board. He felt his body start to sweat, and as he slid his fingers into the tight white collar around his missionary neck he began to pray.

If only he knew what he was praying for.

Scars are precious.

They cost you something – sadness, loss, despair.

But they were born out of something, too.

Born of experience - love, joy, excitement.

Like a tattooed keepsake, your scars will fade

But so will the memories if you let them.

Don't let them go.

They have value.

They are part of you.

And you are breathtaking in every way.

If you enjoyed reading this book, watch out for my new book, Dandelion Drifting, which will be out soon.

If you'd like a sneaky look before it's published, join me at annerobson.com.au.

www.ingramcontent.com/pod-product-compliance
Lightning Source LLC
Chambersburg PA
CBHW072058290426
44110CB00014B/1727